U.S. Fire Administration

Mission Statement

As an entity of the Federal Emergency Management Agency (FEMA), the mission of the U.S. Fire Administration (USFA) is to reduce life and economic losses due to fire and related emergencies, through leadership, advocacy, coordination, and support. We serve the Nation independently, in coordination with other Federal agencies, and in partnership with fire protection and emergency service communities. With a commitment to excellence, we provide public education, training, technology, and data initiatives.

Emerging Health and Safety Issues in the Volunteer Fire Service

March 2008

FEMA

Table of Contents

Introduction

Firefighters, emergency medical technicians (EMTs), and other emergency responders face many dangers daily from exposure to smoke, deadly temperatures, and stress to issues surrounding personal protective equipment (PPE), vehicle safety, and personal health. Although publicized firefighter fatalities are associated more often with burns and smoke inhalation, cardiovascular events, such as sudden cardiac death, account for the largest number of nonincident firefighter fatalities (Fahy, 2005).

Both the United States Fire Administration (USFA) and the National Fire Protection Association (NFPA) have been tracking firefighter fatalities since 1977. According to NFPA statistics, the number of sudden cardiac deaths has averaged between 40 and 50 deaths per year since the early 1990s (Fahy, 2005). USFA statistics show that firefighters, as a group, are more likely than other American workers to die of a heart attack while on duty (USFA, 2002). Additional pertinent findings in the NFPA's 2005 *U.S. Firefighter Fatalities Due to Sudden Cardiac Death, 1995-2004* include

✚ Four hundred and forty firefighters out of 1,006 (or 43.7 percent) who died on the job experienced sudden cardiac death, typically triggered by stress or exertion.

✚ Fifty percent of all volunteer firefighter deaths and 39-percent of career firefighter deaths resulted from a heart attack.

✚ Ninety-seven percent of the victims had at least a 50-percent arterial blockage.

✚ Seventy-five percent of the firefighters who died of a heart attack were working with known or detectable heart conditions or risk factors, such as high cholesterol, high blood pressure, and diabetes.

While sudden cardiac death is the leading cause of death among firefighters, other factors affecting firefighters' health, wellness, and safety result in multiple deaths and injuries each and every year. Through the collection of information on firefighter deaths, the USFA has established goals to reduce loss of life among firefighters (USFA, 2006). In order to achieve this goal, emphasis must be placed on reducing the risk factors associated with cardiovascular disease as well as on the mitigation of other issues affecting the health and safety of the Nation's firefighters.

As part of another effort to determine the specific issues affecting firefighter health and wellness, the National Volunteer Fire Council (NVFC) Foundation developed a questionnaire to determine personal health, well-being, and safety practices among firefighters. A summary of findings from this study was shared with the NVFC and USFA for use in this project. The questionnaire was distributed to a study population of 364 firefighters, of which 149 were career firefighters, 165 were volunteers, and 50 indicated they were both volunteer and career. Results from the questionnaire revealed several trends in this sample firefighter population; however, the study population was not large enough to generalize these trends for all firefighters.

Results from the NVFC Foundation's questionnaire appears on the following pages. Based on these findings, it is clear that a structured personal health and fitness program, as well as safe operations to, from, and while at emergency scenes, become critical to firefighters' safety, well-being, and survival. As a result, we present this document on emergent health and safety issues for the volunteer fire and emergency services.

Personal Health

Blood Pressure

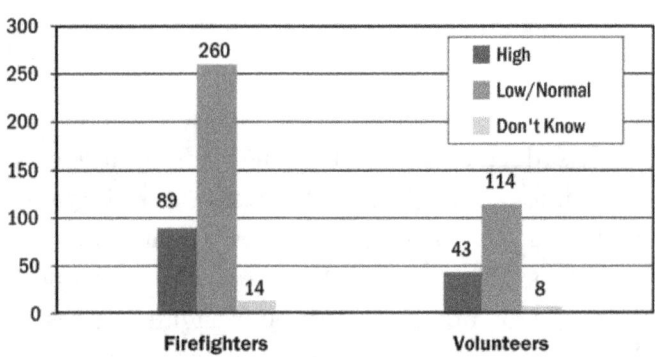

✚ Twenty-five percent of firefighters who responded were told by a doctor or nurse that they have high blood pressure.

Diabetes

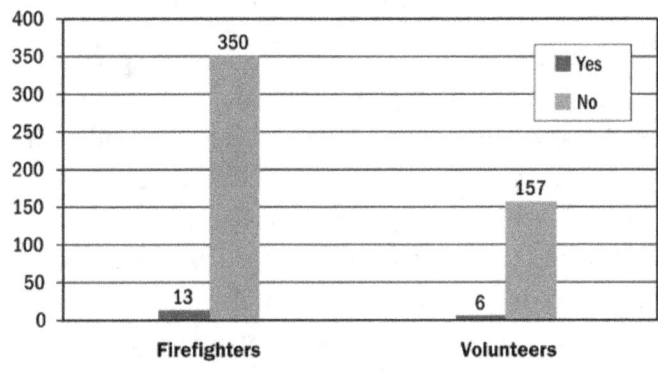

✚ Four percent of firefighters who responded reported having diabetes.

Family History of Heart Disease

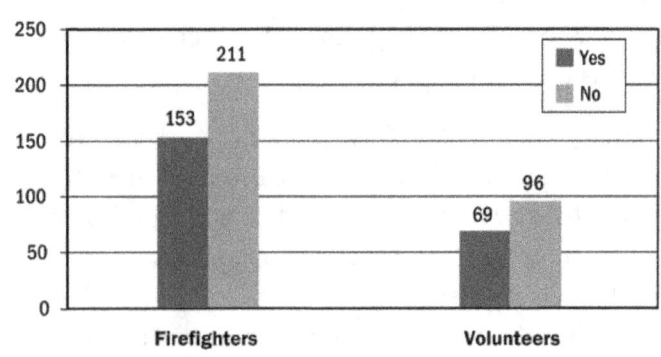

✚ Forty-two percent of firefighters who responded said they have an immediate family member who has suffered a heart attack or stroke.

Heart Attack/Stroke

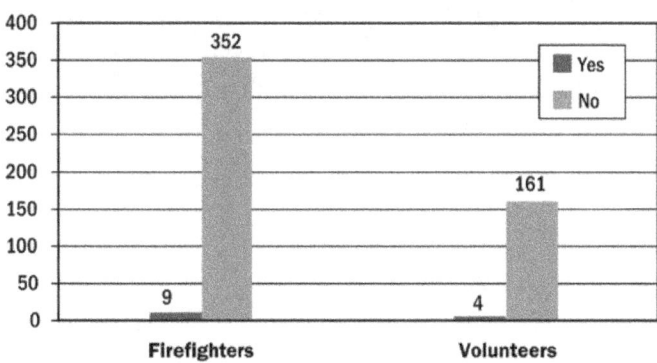

+ Three percent of firefighters who responded reported being told that they have heart disease, or had a stroke or heart attack.

Cholesterol Levels

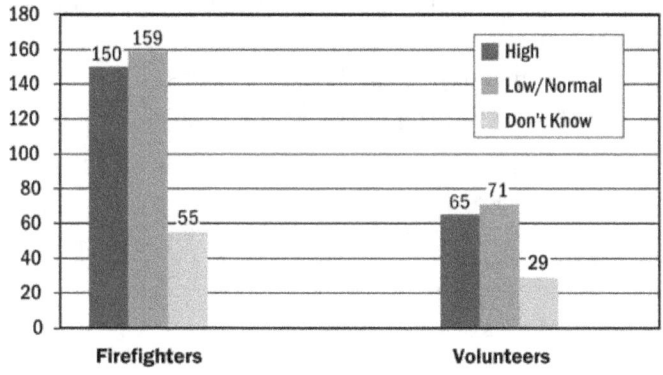

+ Forty percent of firefighters who responded were told by a doctor or nurse that their measured blood cholesterol level was high.

Personal Well-Being

Smoking Status

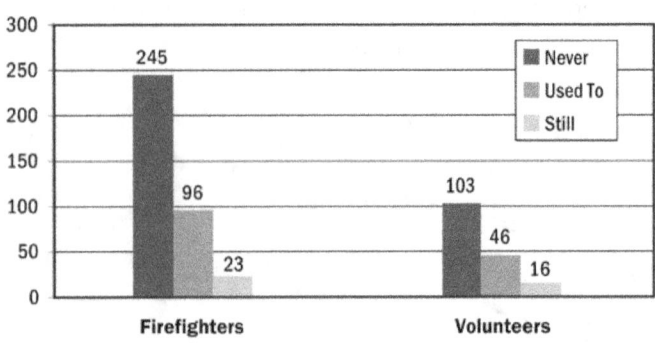

+ Ninety-four percent of firefighters currently are reducing their risk of heart disease, heart attack, high blood pressure, lung cancer, and emphysema and experiencing a higher quality of life by not smoking.

Exercise Frequency

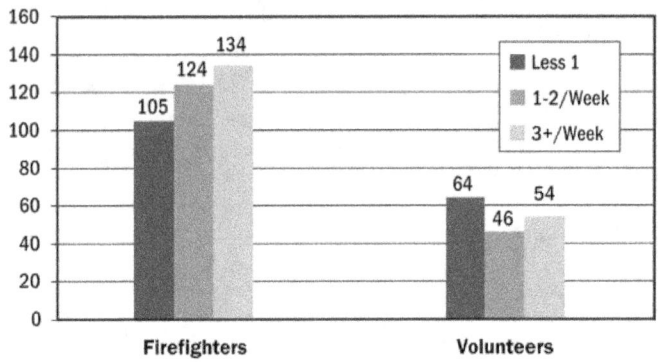

+ Sixty-three percent of firefighters who responded do not meet the Centers for Disease Control and Prevention (CDC) guidelines for leisure-time or physical activity which is 20 to 30 minutes at least three times per week.

Consume Fatty Foods

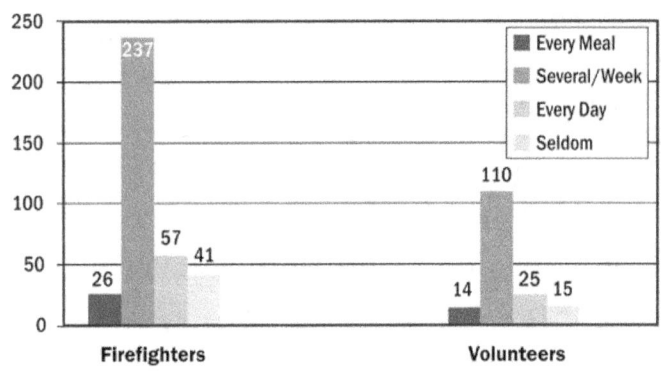

+ Sixty-six percent of firefighters who responded say they consume foods high in saturated fat, such as red meat, whole milk, cheese, and rich desserts several days per week.

Drink and Drive

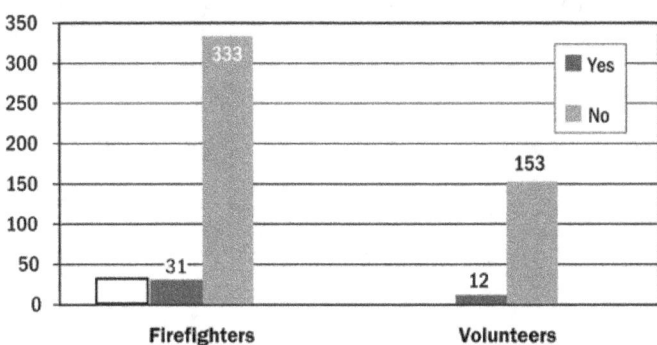

- Eight percent of the firefighters who responded reported driving under the influence of alcohol or riding with a driver under the influence of alcohol.

Feelings of Stress

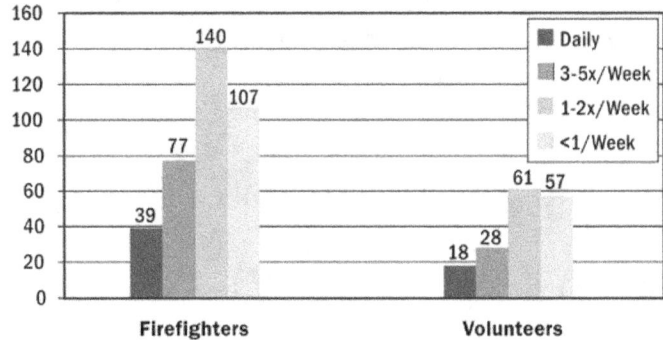

- Thirty-two percent of the firefighters who responded said they feel stressed most days of the week.

Personal Safety

Wear Personal Protective Equipment

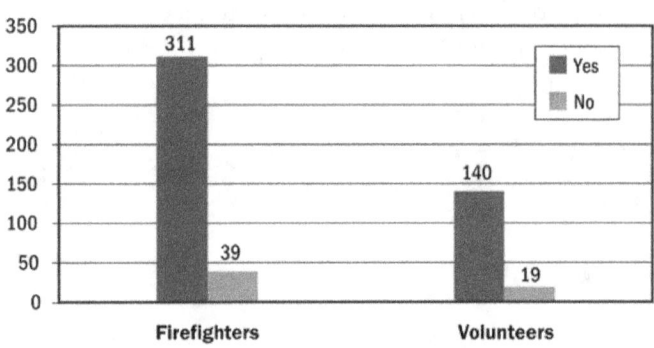

+ Eleven percent of the firefighters who responded indicated that they were not assigned or did not wear PPE.

Consider Fire Vehicles Safe

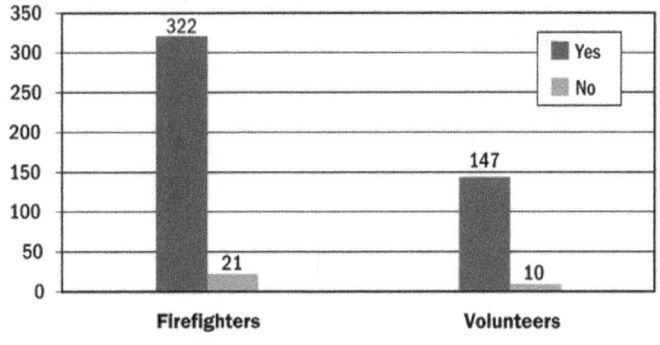

+ Six percent of the firefighters who responded considered their fire vehicles and how they operate the vehicles to be unsafe.

Report Use of Safety Officer

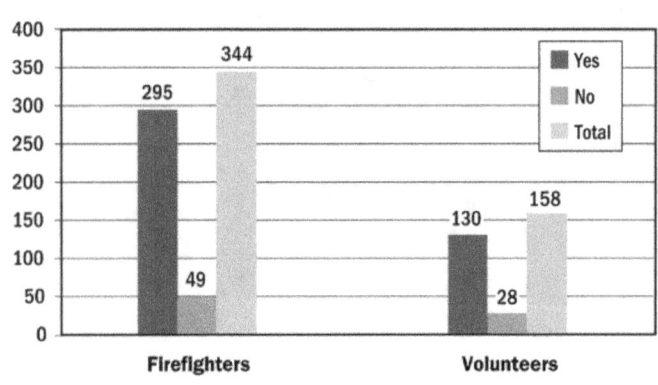

+ Twelve percent of the firefighters who responded indicated their department did not employ a Safety Officer.

Consider Safety Officer Effective

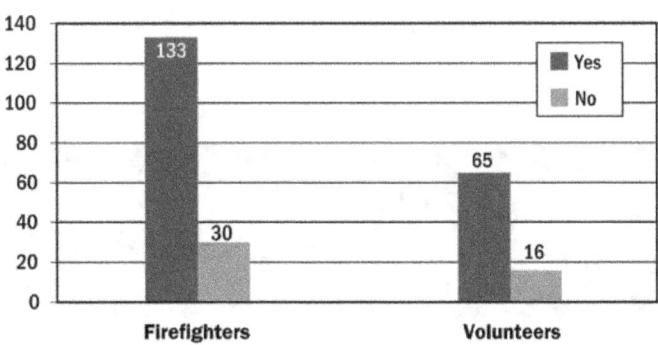

+ Eighteen percent of firefighters who responded indicated that aggressive firefighting actions are taken by their organization when minimal potential for saving lives or property exists.

Report Use of Aggressive Actions

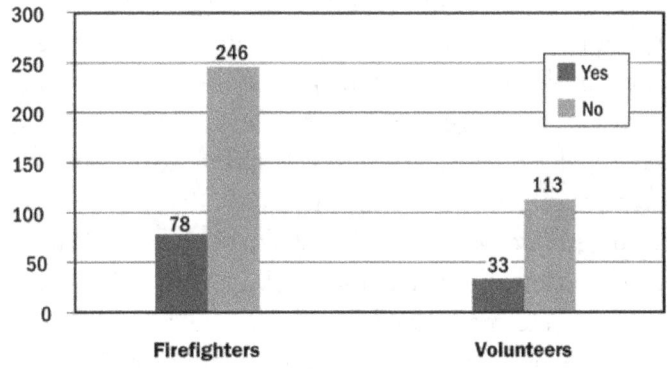

+ Forty-five percent of firefighters who responded indicated poor training as their primary safety concern, and 25 percent of firefighters who responded indicated over-aggressiveness as their primary safety concern.

Emerging Health and Safety Issues

Routine Health Screening		Positive Lifestyle Behaviors		A Safe Work Environment		Reduced Firefighter Fatalities

The results of the NVFC Foundation questionnaire allowed the NVFC and USFA to identify several health and safety issues that are affecting our Nation's firefighters. These emerging issues include health-related factors such as cardiovascular disease, nutrition, physical activity levels, alcohol and tobacco use, diabetes, and stress. Additionally, several safety issues were identified, including safety measures used by fire departments, usage and policies surrounding PPE, and vehicle safety issues. As a Nation, we rely on our emergency responders to protect and save lives and property in times of natural or manmade disasters and other emergencies. In order to do so, they must first be healthy, safe, and able to respond.

The equation above incorporates both individual and societal responsibility for proper health and safety practices. By incorporating the components of this equation into all aspects of the fire service, the NVFC and the USFA hope to reduce firefighter fatalities and injuries and to assist firefighters in becoming healthy, safe, and able to respond to the increasing demands of their communities.

Emerging Health Issues

Findings from the NVFC Foundation questionnaire indicate that the health of firefighters is comparable to the health of the American population. The issues of chronic disease and related risk factors have captured not only the attention of the firefighters, but also the attention of most employers, the Federal government, and the health-care industry because of rising health care costs, decreased productivity, and compromised health status among employees and citizens.

Risk factors predispose individuals for certain chronic diseases and are divided into two categories: modifiable and nonmodifiable. A nonmodifiable risk factor, such as age, gender, or genetics, cannot be changed. Conversely, modifiable risk factors, such as physical activity, tobacco use, and diet, can be changed. Many modifiable risk factors transcend the leading causes of death and disability in the United States. Therefore, improving one's modifiable risk factors—by increasing physical activity or making healthy food choices, for example—could decrease the likelihood of several chronic diseases.

Today, the leading causes of death among all Americans are heart disease, cancer, stroke, diabetes, and smoking-related causes. Management of these problems requires strategies different than those for infectious diseases that were the leading killers during the early part of the last century. Ensuring good health and controlling disease requires a focus on socioeconomic issues (education, work), individual health-related behaviors, the environment, and access to health care. In response, government agencies, organizations, and associations have initiated strategies to manage the rise in chronic disease. The U.S. Department of Health and Human Services (HHS) has set forth *Healthy People 2010*, a comprehensive document with a strategic plan for the health of this Nation (2005); organizations have been active in implementing wellness programs for employees and members (Peregrin, 2005; Schult, McGovern, Dowd, and Pronk, 2006); and associations have been involved actively in raising awareness among professionals (Brundtland, 2002; Position of the American Dietetic Association, 1989, 1998). Collectively, these efforts are gaining momentum although there is still much more work to be done.

The emergence of health promotion was in response to the rise in chronic disease resulting from increased rates of obesity and smoking, sedentary behaviors, and stress in our society. Health promotion is defined as the science and art of helping people make changes in their lifestyle to move toward a state of optimal health (O'Donnell and Ainsworth, 1984). Lifestyle change can be facilitated through a combination of efforts that enhance awareness, change behavior, and create environments that support good health practices (O'Donnell and Ainsworth, 1984). By eating healthy foods, maintaining a proper weight, engaging in regular physical activity, and participating in health screenings, firefighters can do their part in being proactive in their fight against cardiovascular disease and other leading chronic diseases.

We will begin by addressing the leading chronic diseases and the modifiable risk factors related to firefighters' health. Following this, we have proposed goals for reducing these health risks and program and policy strategies for addressing them, ultimately leading to a reduction in chronic disease.

Emerging Health Issue: Cardiovascular Disease

In the United States, more than 61 million men and women suffer some form of heart and blood vessel disease, and many die from these diseases (HHS, 2005). Cardiovascular disease (CVD) is the leading cause of death in the United States. At one time CVD was considered to affect men only; however, heart disease among women is on the rise. Further, because CVD is a progressive disease and may start

early in a person's life, children are now being screened for selected risk factors (i.e., cholesterol) that may predispose them to CVD.

CVD begins with the process of atherosclerosis, characterized by plaques along the inner walls of the arteries. The formation of plaque eventually decreases the diameter of the artery wall, decreasing the blood flow throughout the body. Further, these plaques create hypertension and trigger abnormal clotting of the blood, leading to heart attacks and strokes.

The causes of plaque formation are very complex and involve foods consumed, inflammatory response to tissue damage, and a host of other compounds in the blood. There is a considerable amount of research being conducted to understand the etiology of disease, strategies for reducing risk behavior, and pharmaceutical and surgical approaches to treat this.

National efforts to fight CVD have led to discoveries about prevention, screening, and health promotion. An expert panel of the National Cholesterol Education Program defined major heart disease risk factors, which include increasing age, male gender, family history, high blood low-density lipoproteins (LDL) cholesterol, low blood high-density lipoproteins (HDL) cholesterol, high blood pressure, diabetes, obesity, physical inactivity, and cigarette-smoking. Age, gender, and family history cannot be modified, whereas the remaining factors can be modified through behavior change programs that decrease heart disease risks.

With the proper knowledge and skills, individuals have the opportunity to make appropriate health changes to reduce risk factors. Fortunately, there are several modifiable risk factors related to CVD, allowing an individual opportunities to decrease his or her risk.

In 1984, high blood cholesterol levels were established as a risk factor for CVD. Further research has focused on LDL and HDL. LDL is "bad" cholesterol because it carries cholesterol to cells that line the arteries, where it can become part of the plaques of atherosclerosis. The higher the LDL level is, the greater the risk of CVD. HDL is "good" cholesterol because it carries cholesterol away from the cells to the liver. Elevated HDL indicates a reduced risk of atherosclerosis. High LDL and low HDL correlate directly with heart disease.

Hypertension is another modifiable risk factor for CVD. The higher the blood pressure is above the recommended normal reading, the greater the risk of heart attack or stroke. Hypertension injures the artery walls and accelerates plaque formation, thus initiating or worsening the progression of atherosclerosis. High blood pressure transcends age and gender as a risk factor for CVD and should be treated aggressively. Twenty-five percent of firefighters who responded to the questionnaire indicated they had been diagnosed with high blood pressure, making it a particular concern among the modifiable risk factors.

Diabetes constitutes a major independent risk factor for all forms of CVD, substantially increasing other risks. With diabetes, atherosclerosis progresses rapidly, blocking blood vessels and diminishing circulation. For diabetics, the risk of a future heart attack is roughly equal to that of a person with confirmed heart disease, and the consequences are likely to be severe.

Cigarette-smoking is a powerful risk factor for heart disease. The more a person smokes, the higher the CVD risk, a fact that transcends gender-related risks. Smoking directly damages the heart with toxins and burdens it by raising blood pressure. Due to reduced oxygen when individuals smoke, the heart must work harder to deliver blood, thereby increasing the heart's workload. Smoking also damages platelets, making blood clots likely. When people quit smoking, their risk of heart disease begins to drop within a few months; hence, the effect is immediate and further reduces risk over time.

Obesity and physical inactivity are the last two modifiable risk factors associated with CVD. Obesity, especially obesity around a person's middle, and physical inactivity amplify a person's risk for CVD by elevating LDL cholesterol, lowering HDL cholesterol, and worsening hypertension and diabetes. Conversely, weight loss and physical activity lower LDL and raise HDL cholesterol, improve insulin function, and lower blood pressure.

Emerging Health Issue: Nutrition

Nutrition factors play a role in four of the leading causes of death in the United States. These factors include excess consumption of dietary cholesterol, fat, sodium, and sugar and inadequate consumption of fiber. After smoking, obesity is the second leading cause of preventable death in the United States. Our questionnaire inquired about one nutrition behavior—the consumption of fatty foods. Sixty-six percent of firefighters who responded reported consuming foods high in saturated fat, such as red meat, whole milk, cheese, and rich desserts, several days per week. Height and weight data were not collected to calculate Body Mass Index (BMI) in order to document the rates of being overweight or obese. In the future, health surveys might inquire about these data points.

Cholesterol is a risk factor for CVD, as mentioned in the previous section. Cholesterol is produced by the body and consumed in foods (animal products only). Blood cholesterol is raised by a high intake of saturated fats, also found primarily in animal products. Foods rich in saturated fat and cholesterol include whole-milk dairy products, pork, and beef. Fats found in these foods are said to be "hidden" fats since they are less visible to people. Processed foods such as potato chips, cookies, pastries, and other snack foods may contain "trans-fat," a type of fat that also raises blood cholesterol levels. Total fat intake is also a nutritional concern because of saturated fats and the amount of calories contained in high-fat foods. Regular consumption of high-fat foods may increase a person's caloric intake, resulting in weight gain over time. The NVFC Foundation questionnaire inquired about elevated cholesterol levels. Forty percent of firefighters who responded indicated they had been told by a medical professional that they had high cholesterol.

An increased intake of sodium, an electrolyte, may cause an increase in an individual's blood pressure. When an individual has hypertension (as 25 percent of respondents reported on the NVFC Foundation questionnaire), it is recommended they follow a low-sodium diet, or the DASH (Dietary Approaches to Stop Hypertension) diet. This diet encourages the consumption of fewer processed foods, which contain a significant amount of sodium, and more whole grains, fruits, and vegetables, as well as more homemade meals, since they contain less sodium than those prepared at restaurants.

Sugar is a simple carbohydrate and is used to sweeten foods. Over the past decade many other sweeteners, such as high-fructose corn syrup, also have become part of our food supply. People with diets high in added sugars may consume more calories, and this may lead to weight gain. Further, individuals may replace nutrient-rich beverages, like milk, with sugared beverages, like soda, resulting in the consumption of fewer nutrients. Individuals with Type-2 diabetes must limit their sugar intake. While sugar eaten in moderation has not been shown to be harmful, practicing moderation has been challenging for consumers.

Fiber is the indigestible parts of plant foods. Fiber is found in whole grain items (whole wheat bread or fiber-rich cereal), fruits, and vegetables. Fiber is recognized for many important roles in maintaining good health. First, it is known to reduce blood-cholesterol levels and is therefore related to decreasing the risk for CVD. Second, it increases insulin sensitivity, thereby assisting those with Type-2 diabetes. Populations consuming a high-fiber diet generally have lower rates of colon cancer than comparable populations (Whitney and Rolfes, 2008). Lastly, foods rich in fiber tend to be low in fat and added sugars, thus promoting weight loss by delivering fewer calories per bite.

Obesity is a precursor to many chronic diseases including CVD, cancer, stroke, hypertension, and diabetes. The rising rates of obesity in the United States clearly indicate that steps need to be taken to address this risk factor. Unfortunately, obesity is a complex problem that requires a multi-faceted approach involving both personal commitment and environmental changes. However, if an overweight person loses just 10-percent of his or her body weight, he or she will see positive changes in blood pressure, blood cholesterol, and glucose levels.

Emerging Health Issue: Physical Activity

Regular physical activity offers many benefits to individual health. Aerobic, endurance-type activities, such as brisk walking, undertaken for 30 minutes on a regular basis (three or more days per week) will strengthen the heart and blood vessels, improve body composition, and lower blood pressure and blood cholesterol. These changes are so beneficial that some experts believe that physical activity should be the primary focus of heart disease prevention efforts (Berlin and Colditz, 1990) and other chronic diseases (Booth and Lees, 2007; Warburton, Nicol, and Bredin, 2006).

Physical activity is divided into the following four areas:

1. **Flexibility**—the ability of the joints to move through a full range of motion.

2. **Muscular strength**—the ability of the muscles to exert force for a brief period of time.

3. **Muscular endurance**—the ability of the muscle to perform repetitive movements.

4. **Cardiorespiratory endurance**—the ability of the body to supply fuel during extended periods of moderate-to-high intensity bouts of exercise.

In order to improve each area listed above, different exercises should be incorporated into an exercise regimen. For example, stretching will improve flexibility; weight training will improve muscular strength and endurance; and aerobic activity, such as running, cycling, or swimming will improve cardiorespiratory endurance. In order to develop an effective exercise regimen, it is necessary to consider the number of times an exercise is performed per unit of time (frequency), the percent of one's maximum heart rate at which the exercise is performed (intensity), and the length of time each exercise is performed (duration).

Using this information, specific guidelines to increase one's fitness level are outlined below:

A more realistic goal for the majority of Americans is to incorporate enough physical activity into each day

	Cardiorespiratory	Strength	Flexibility
Frequency	3 to 5 days per week	2 to 3 days per week	2 to 3 days per week
Intensity	Target heart rate range (55 to 90 percent of maximum heart rate or [(220−age)×0.55×0.90]	Varies; enough to increase muscular strength and body composition	Varies; enough to develop a full range of motion
Duration	20 to 60 minutes	8 to 10 repetitions of 8 to 10 different exercises	4 repetitions of 10 to 30 seconds per muscle group

to maintain a healthy body weight. The CDC recommends physical activity of 20 to 30 minutes at least three days per week. In 2005, the world's largest ongoing telephone health survey system found that only 51 percent of 25- to 34-year-olds, 49.6 percent of 35- to 44-year-olds, and 46 percent of 45- to 64-year-olds were meeting these recommendations (CDC, 2006). Unfortunately, the results of the NVFC Foundation's questionnaire revealed an even higher percentage than the national average. Sixty-three percent of firefighters who responded do not meet the current recommendations.

It is possible to meet the CDC's guidelines for exercise by integrating physical activity into leisure time activities. For instance, dusting, vacuuming, and gardening are considered light-intensity activities; lawn mowing, scrubbing floors, and washing windows are considered moderate-intensity activities, and moving furniture, playing singles tennis, and jogging are considered vigorous-intensity activities. Realizing that less time needs to be spent on moderate- and vigorous-intensity activities also will help maximize the amount of time allotted for exercise.

Emerging Health Issue: *Alcohol Abuse*

According to the National Institute on Alcohol Abuse and Alcoholism, 14 million Americans meet standard criteria for alcohol abuse or alcoholism. Further, alcohol plays a role in one in four cases of violent crime, and more than 16,000 people die each year in automobile accidents that involve alcohol. Alcohol abuse costs more than $180 billion dollars a year (National Institute on Drug Abuse, 2007). No data were collected on alcohol consumption for firefighters on the NVFC Foundation questionnaire; however, its inclusion might be considered for the future.

Excessive alcohol intake has been shown to raise the levels of triglycerides in the blood and lead to high blood pressure and heart failure. When more than the recommended amount of alcohol (two drinks per day for men and one drink per day for women) is consumed, the risk of alcoholism, high blood pressure, obesity, stroke, breast cancer, suicide, and accidents increases (Alcohol, Wine and Cardiovascular Disease, n.d.).

Most health assessments are based on self-report information, and individuals tend to underreport negative habits. The only alcohol-related behavior addressed in the NVFC Foundation questionnaire was drinking and driving, with eight percent of the firefighters surveyed having reported driving under the influence of alcohol or riding with a driver under the influence of alcohol. Although this percentage is low, future efforts should be focused on reducing this percentage to zero. Additionally, the health concerns of alcohol consumption warrant including some questions about its use and possible abuse in a future health survey.

Emerging Health Issue: *Tobacco Use*

Tobacco use accounts for more than 440,000 deaths annually (HHS, 2005). It is the number one preventable cause of death in the United States today. Although rates have decreased as a result of no-smoking policies and increased taxes, approximately 21 percent of Americans smoke. The NVFC Foundation questionnaire found that only four percent of firefighters reported to be smokers. Again, it is important to note that individuals tend to underreport negative behaviors and habits.

Smoking increases the chances of getting many different forms of cancer, as well as being a risk factor for other chronic diseases. Lung cancer is the most common kind of cancer caused by smoking. A smoker is at greater risk of getting cancer of the lips, mouth, throat, or voice box. Smokers also have a higher risk of getting esophagus, stomach, kidney, pancreas, cervix, bladder, and skin cancer. Smoking is a major risk factor for CVD. If smokers have heart or blood vessel problems and they smoke, they are at even greater risk of having continued or worse health problems. Cigarette smoke increases blood clotting and may damage the lining of the heart's arteries and other blood vessels. Lastly, smokers are at high risk for lung disease. The younger a person is when he or she begins smoking, the greater the risk of getting lung disease. This is evidenced by the cough many smokers have, caused by the chemicals in smoke. Moreover, depending upon how much one smokes, the lungs become gray and "dirty" (they look like charcoal), whereas healthy lungs are pink.

There are many organizations and local, State, and Federal government policies that prohibit smoking in buildings. These policies create clean indoor air for nonsmokers and underscore the need for policies to support healthy living. Clinical interventions are available to people who want to stop smoking. Many of these interventions are initiated with the assistance of a physician who can prescribe nicotine-replacement therapies and provide access to "help-lines" to assist the smoker in quitting.

Emerging Health Issue: Diabetes

Diabetes is the fastest growing chronic disease in the United States. Of all the children and adults in the United States, 20.8 million, or 7 percent of the population, have diabetes. While an estimated 14.6 million have been diagnosed with diabetes, 6.2 million people (or nearly one-third) are unaware that they have the disease (National Diabetes Information Clearinghouse, 2005). Four percent of the firefighters who responded to the NVFC Foundation questionnaire reported having been diagnosed with diabetes.

Diabetes is a disease in which the body either does not produce or properly use insulin. The role of insulin is to facilitate the removal of blood glucose from the blood and transport it into cells for the body to use as energy. When blood glucose remains in the blood stream, this condition is called "hyperglycemia." Prolonged hyperglycemia causes a number of systematic complications involving many parts of the body. Some complications of Type-2 diabetes include heart disease (cardiovascular disease), blindness (retinopathy), nerve damage (neuropathy), and kidney damage (nephropathy).

The most predominant type of diabetes is Type-2 diabetes. People with Type-2 diabetes tend to be obese, which can cause or exacerbate insulin resistance. Risk factors for Type-2 diabetes include two nonmodifiable risk factors, family history and age, and two modifiable risk factors, obesity and physical inactivity. Physicians now routinely screen for diabetes, and estimates indicate that 54 million Americans have pre-diabetes. This group is strongly encouraged to reduce their weight and initiate an exercise program.

Nutrition and physical activity interventions play a central role in managing diabetes, with a focus on weight control in Type-2 diabetes. Nutritional plans should take into consideration overall caloric intake, increasing complex carbohydrates (e.g., whole-wheat bread) while reducing simple sugars (e.g., soda), and decreasing saturated fat (animal fat) to reduce the risk of CVD. Regular cardiovascular exercise is a key strategy to achieving and maintaining a healthy body weight, but it has been shown to increase tissue sensitivity to insulin also.

Emerging Health Issue: Stress Management

The NVFC Foundation's findings revealed that 32 percent of the respondents reported feeling stressed most days of the week. According to medical research, as much as 90 percent of illness and disease can be related to stress. Stress interferes with physical functioning and bodily processes and has been linked to high blood pressure and cardiovascular disease, as well as insomnia, ulcers, and rashes (Stress Management for the Health of It, n.d.). Stress is a physiological response to an event that may cause either positive or negative feelings within us. It is the "wear and tear" one's body experiences as it adjusts to a continually changing environment. Stress can be felt from a major life-changing event (e.g., job change) or from small events throughout a day (e.g., traffic). Further, stress is highly personalized, and events that may be stressful to one person may not affect another person. Therefore, stress management needs to be personalized to individuals. Fortunately, a plethora of methods used to help people manage their stress exists, such as meditation, visual imagery, and progressive relaxation, among others.

Emerging Safety Issues

While physical/personal health issues historically account for 50 percent of firefighter deaths annually, the remaining 50 percent deal with what can be termed as occupational safety issues. There is a need to identify these issues and their associated best practices in an effort to mitigate the emerging issues of PPE use, safe design and operation of emergency vehicles, use of a safety officer, and proactively determining and addressing local safety issues. In all cases, the standard safety engineering approach, "Basic Measures for Preventing Accidental Injury" as defined in the National Safety Council's Accident Prevention Manual for Industrial Operations, applies to the fire service as an approach to controlling accident potential and fatalities (1978). This four-step approach includes

1. Attempt to eliminate the hazard from the machine, method, material, or structure.

2. Control the hazard by enclosing or guarding it at its source.

3. Train personnel to be aware of the hazard and to follow safe job procedures to avoid it (including Standard Operating Procedures (SOPs)/Standard Operating Guidelines (SOGs).

4. Prescribe PPE for personnel to shield them against the hazard.

Emerging Safety Issue: Safety Measures

The Occupational Safety and Health Administration (OSHA), along with business and industry leaders, have advocated safety programs for more than 30 years as a method not only of protecting oneself in the workplace, but also at home, at leisure, and on the fireground. Safety practices include engineering out the problem, providing PPE when a safety problem cannot be engineered out, and using administrative practices (e.g., training and SOPs) to supplement PPE and engineering safeguards—(National Safety Council, 1978).

The NVFC Foundation questionnaire found that 45 percent of the respondents indicated poor training as their primary safety concern, while 25 percent indicated over-aggressiveness as their primary safety concern. Both of these findings lead to a concern about the leadership and structure of training as well as safety policies and practices. Leadership of the organization must remember that establishing a culture of safe operations is the primary way to instill a constant awareness of personal safety and practices. As noted above, this arises through an attempt to "engineer-out" as many hazardous situations as possible, in addition to the development of policies and procedures that indicate the proper way to conduct various tasks and when to avoid a potentially dangerous situation, as well as training for when and how to use various tools and related PPE. This approach, used in the safety engineering discipline, has been the primary method used by OSHA to eliminate accidents, injuries, and illnesses in the general workplace and can be adopted easily into the fire service. In addition, the National Institute for Occupational Safety and Health's (NIOSH), Fire Fighter Fatality Investigation and Prevention Program (FFFIPP) which investigates all line-of-duty deaths of firefighters, continually finds the lack of SOPs, proper supervision, training, and the use of PPE as the primary contributors of firefighter line-of-duty deaths.

Similarly, there is a concern regarding over-aggressiveness on the fireground. This relates to two major issues.

1. The attempt to enter a property or incident scene for rescue or firefighting when there is no potential for saving a life or the structure's damage from the fire is too significant to be handled swiftly and easily without putting firefighters in considerable harm's way—in other words, risking more than there is to save.

2. The same can be said for responding at too fast a rate of speed for road, highway, or incident conditions. Speeding (overaggressive driving) is a major contributor to firefighter deaths and injury according to the analysis of fire apparatus accidents.

All of these situations are local in nature and solution. While there are SOGs that are generic in scope and promoted nationally, they must be modified to the local community, matched to local issues and problems, and preplanning information must be integrated into the development of SOPs to provide as safe a workplace as possible for firefighters.

Emerging Safety Issue: Personal Protective Equipment

PPE is designed as a second level of protection when the hazard cannot be engineered out of the workplace. In the case of firefighters, it is designed both to prevent injury or illness (by limiting the impact of a hazard on the body), and to ensure loss reduction (by lessening the impact of injury or illness when it occurs). Today's PPE for firefighters is capable of providing full body protection and has been known to save lives. However, proper care, maintenance, and use of the PPE is critical to optimal performance (VFIS, 2000). Results from the NVFC Foundation questionnaire indicate that 11 percent of respondents were not assigned or were not required to wear their PPE.

Emerging Safety Issue: Vehicle Safety

Year after year, approximately 25 percent of the firefighters who are killed in the line of duty are responding to or returning from incidents, with the majority of the fatalities resulting from vehicle crashes. This represents the second leading cause of firefighter fatalities (NVFC, 2005). Investigations have found a consistent pattern of driver error, vehicle maintenance, speed, and the lack of seatbelt use to be among the contributing factors. Additionally, numerous firefighters have died working at emergency sites after being struck by vehicles. Death, although the most devastating, is only one area of concern. Collisions cause injuries, which can be more costly than death in terms of long-term pain, suffering, and expense. The NVFC Foundation questionnaire found that 21 percent of the respondents reported their vehicles to be unsafe due to inadequate training, inadequate maintenance, nonenclosed seating, and non-SOPs.

Emerging Safety Issue: Safety Officers

Over the past two decades, the staffing of Safety Officers has been introduced and ingrained within the fire service as an effective method to manage the safe operations of the fire department in the station, en route and returning from incidents, as well as at the incident itself. Today's more cautious approach includes not taking unnecessary risks while conducting the job safely and efficiently. The role of the Safety Officer is critical in the ultimate effectiveness of the safety measures described earlier. The NVFC Foundation questionnaire found that 12 percent of the respondents indicated that their department did not employ Safety Officers. Disabilities and deaths of firefighters should not be an expected part of the job, and as such, Safety Officers play a prominent role as the champion, developer, implementer, and monitor of safe working conditions. The failure to assign someone as a Safety Officer will create a significant void in the ultimate effectiveness of safety in the workplace.

Goals and Objectives

The American Heart Association (AHA), in cooperation with the Centers for Disease Control and Prevention (CDC) and the Department of Health and Human Services (HHS), created a Public Health Action Plan to Reduce Heart Disease and Stroke in 2003. This plan incorporates *Healthy People 2010* goals and objectives in order to improve cardiovascular health and reduce the risk of coronary heart disease in the United States. It identifies three components for reducing heart attack and stroke: (1) the prevention, detection, and treatment of risk factors; (2) the early identification and treatment of heart attack and stroke; and (3) the prevention of recurrent cardiovascular events.

Although the risk factors for coronary heart disease are modifiable, their prevalence continues to increase in the American population. These risk factors are also evident in many of the 364 firefighters who responded to the questionnaire. In order to combat the increased incidence of these risk factors, particularly in the fire service, a strategy must be developed. This strategy may be similar to those outlined in the *Public Health Action Plan to Reduce Heart Disease and Stroke* (CDC, 2003) and *Healthy People 2010* (HHS, 2005). These plans identify measurable goals and objectives for reversing risk factors and sudden cardiac death among at-risk populations. Additionally, measurable goals and objectives must be identified for combating other emerging health, safety, and wellness issues among our Nation's firefighters.

"The health of an individual is almost inseparable from the health of the larger community and the health of every community determines the overall health status of the nation" (HHS, 2005). In an effort to ensure the health and safety of firefighters who are called upon every day to protect our neighbors, our families, and our communities, the NVFC and USFA identify the following measurable goals and objectives:

Goal: Combat Heart Disease

ISSUE: Of firefighter deaths in 2005, 47.8 percent resulted from heart attack (USFA, 2006).

OBJECTIVE: Reduce coronary heart disease deaths by 20 percent (*Healthy People* 2010, 12-1).

Goal: Reduce Blood Cholesterol Levels

ISSUE: Forty-one percent of firefighters who responded to the NVFC Foundation questionnaire reported having high total blood cholesterol levels.

OBJECTIVE: Reduce mean total blood cholesterol levels among all firefighters to less than 200 mg/dL (*Healthy People* 2010, 12-13).

OBJECTIVE: Reduce the proportion of firefighters with high total blood cholesterol levels to 17 percent.

OBJECTIVE: Achieve a proportion of 80 percent of firefighters who have had their blood cholesterol levels checked within the preceding five years.

Goal: Reduce Blood Pressure

ISSUE: Twenty-five percent of the firefighters who responded reported having high blood pressure.

OBJECTIVE: Reduce the number of firefighters with high blood pressure to 16 percent (*Healthy People 2010*, 12-9).

OBJECTIVE: Increase the proportion of all firefighters with high blood pressure whose blood pressure is under control to 50 percent of all firefighters (*Healthy People 2010*, 12-10).

OBJECTIVE: Increase the proportion of all firefighters with high blood pressure who are taking action (losing weight, increasing physical activity, and reducing sodium intake) to help control their blood pressure to 95 percent (*Healthy People 2010*, 12-11).

OBJECTIVE: Increase the proportion of all firefighters who can state whether their blood pressure is normal or high to 95 percent (*Healthy People 2010*, 12-12).

Goal: Decrease Diabetes

ISSUE: Four percent of firefighters who responded reported being diagnosed with diabetes.

OBJECTIVE: Ensure firefighters diagnosed with diabetes receive formal diabetes education (*Healthy People 2010*, 5-1).

Goal: Increase Regular Physical Activity

ISSUE: Twenty-seven percent of firefighters who responded reported engaging in regular physical activity.

OBJECTIVE: Increase the number of firefighters who engage in regular, preferably daily, moderate physical activity for at least 30 minutes per day to 30 percent (*Healthy People 2010*, 22-2).

Goal: Encourage Personal Protective Equipment Use

ISSUE: Eleven percent of firefighters reported that they were not assigned, or did not wear, PPE, with over 65 percent not required to wear it even when assigned.

OBJECTIVE: Increase the number of firefighters who are provided, wear, and are required to wear PPE to 100 percent (NFPA 1500, *Standard on Fire Department Occupational Safety and Health Program*).

Goal: Increase Safe Vehicle Operation

ISSUE: Six percent of firefighters who responded reported their vehicles to be unsafe due to inadequate training, inadequate maintenance, nonenclosed seating, and non-SOPs.

OBJECTIVE: Decrease the number of firefighters who consider their vehicles to be unsafe by implementing a comprehensive vehicle safety program for their organization.

Goal: Increase the Number of Safety Officers

ISSUE: Forty-nine percent of firefighters reported the absence of a Safety Officer in their department.

OBJECTIVE: Work toward ensuring all fire departments have an assigned or functioning Safety Officer.

Goal: Decrease Aggressive Firefighting Actions

ISSUE: Eighteen percent of firefighters reported that their organization took aggressive firefighting actions when no life-saving objectives existed and there was minimal potential for saving significant property.

OBJECTIVE: Ensure organizations no longer take unnecessary actions when there is no life-saving objective or minimal potential for saving significant property.

Goal: Increase Knowledge of Safety Issues

ISSUE: Forty-six percent of firefighters reported their safety training as poor, and 25 percent of firefighters indicated overaggressive behavior that could potentially adversely affect safety and contribute to accidents, injuries, death, and property damage.

OBJECTIVE: Increase the number of firefighters who are trained properly, and work toward eliminating the number of firefighters who are overaggressive in operations by performing evaluations locally and taking appropriate action.

Best Practice Solutions

A best practice is defined as "a technique or methodology that, through experience and research, has proven to reliably lead to a desired result" (TJIS, 2004).

The Wellness Council of America (WELCOA) has developed seven steps that are considered to be the "science" behind building a comprehensive health and wellness initiative ("Seven Benchmarks," n.d.) These seven steps are the foundation of successful health promotion programs and can be applied to health, wellness, and safety issues in the fire service as follows:

Step I. Securing Senior Fire Service Leadership Support within the fire service is critical to its success. Active endorsement and promotion by senior fire service leadership is necessary for the development of a sustainable and successful health, wellness, and safety program. A clear and ongoing message of support from senior officials will legitimize the importance and initiatives of the program, as well as encourage full participation among the ranks.

The goals and objectives that are established for the health, wellness, and safety program must align with the short- and long-term strategies of the fire service. If not, firefighters and fire service leaders will view the program as irrelevant and unimportant. In order to secure and maintain support for the program, senior leadership must embrace the program, actively engage in the program, and clearly communicate its tangible benefits. In this way, all firefighters will realize the value of the program.

Step II. Create a Cohesive Health, Wellness, and Safety Committee/Team that will help maintain and expand the initiative within the fire service. In order to reach the more than one million firefighters in the United States successfully, it may be necessary to appoint regional health, wellness, and safety teams that can coordinate efforts to promote participation in these programs.

Each regional wellness team should consist of a representative sample of the population being served. Collectively, their passion and dedication to the goals of the health, wellness, and safety program will help ensure its success. Additionally, members of the team who have recovered from or experienced the medical or safety conditions targeted by the program can provide valuable testimonials.

A group of 8 to 15 people is small enough to allow meaningful participation by each person and large enough to generate realistic ideas for success. The duties of the health, wellness, and safety team are to establish:

✚ a vision that drives the team;

✚ tangible goals and effective communication of these goals; and

✚ roles and responsibilities.

Step III. Create an Operating Plan. All quality organizational initiatives operate from detailed, focused, outcome-oriented plans. The regional health, wellness, and safety teams should work together to establish an effective plan that includes:

✚ SMART (specific, measurable, achievable, realistic, time-specific) objectives;

✚ implementation strategies and timeline;

✚ marketing and communication procedures;

+ budget;

+ evaluation plan; and

+ future vision of the program.

Ultimately, the regional health, wellness, and safety teams are responsible for implementing the plan and charting the progress of the program. The operating plan is, therefore, a vital instrument for ensuring continued participation and financial support for the program.

Step IV. Choose Appropriate Interventions.
Funding resources will determine the scope of the health, wellness, and safety program. With sufficient funding, multiple delivery methods can be used to promote and reinforce the importance of the program. It is commonly known that individuals need to hear a message nine separate times before they will take appropriate action.

The AHA, HHS, and the CDC all agree that lifestyle interventions that promote heart-healthy behaviors are a major strategy in reducing the incidence and development of coronary heart disease. Similarly, even a physically fit firefighter can be injured, disabled, or killed if safety practices are not integrated into daily routines. Any intervention program developed and delivered to fire service personnel should incorporate, either through awareness or action, the following preventive measures:

+ CHOLESTEROL: Eating a diet low in total fat, saturated fat, and dietary cholesterol, along with physical activity and weight control, can lower cholesterol levels (*High Blood Cholesterol Prevention*, n.d.).

+ PHYSICAL ACTIVITY: Engaging in regular physical or leisure-activity produces health benefits and lowers the risk for coronary heart disease (Berlin and Colditz, 1990).

+ BLOOD PRESSURE: Increasing physical activity, reducing sodium intake, maintaining a healthy weight, and eating a diet high in fruits and vegetables may reduce blood pressure levels (*Healthy Lifestyle*, 2006).

+ DIABETES: Engaging in regular physical activity and maintaining a healthy weight can reduce the risk for diabetes (*Can Type-2 Diabetes Be Prevented?*, n.d.).

+ SAFETY: Safety experts have long attributed six management interventions as critical to performing safe operations. These include

   1. Employee selection and hiring.

   2. Provide appropriate introductory and refresher training.

   3. Establishing, training in, and enforcing safe operating procedures.

   4. Providing protective equipment as necessary.

   5. Investigating accidents and taking action to prevent reoccurrence.

   6. Avoiding the act if it places the individual in a situation where there is little or no chance of a successful outcome.

Some examples of interventions that the fire service can incorporate are

+ The **Know Your Numbers** campaign uses purchased incentives, such as red "LiveLong" bracelets, that are distributed to fire service personnel who know their blood pressure, cholesterol, and glucose numbers. The bracelets have space to imprint these measurements.

+ The **Fired Up for Fitness Challenge** is a regional/statewide challenge for all firefighters (and families) that offers incentives for participation and provides recognition of completion (*http://challenge. healthy-firefighter.org/*).

+ The **NVFC Heart-Healthy Firefighter Program** promotes health awareness and education, fitness, and nutrition through an interactive Web site, (*www. healthy-firefighter.org*), a monthly electronic newsletter, "Heart-Healthy Firefighter Resource Guide," and a Heart-Healthy cookbook (*www.nvfc.org*).

+ The **Sounding the Alarm for High Cholesterol** campaign challenges firefighters and EMS personnel to learn more about high cholesterol and its role in heart disease through a fun and interactive quiz (www.cholesterolalarm.com).

+ The *Awareness Campaign* offers point-of-decision prompts. These prompts are displayed prominently in fire houses and remind firefighters to breathe deeply, to exercise, or to take a stretch break.

+ Provide an exercise area in each fire station with basic equipment that emphasizes both core and functional strength. Equipment should include, but not be limited to, small free weights, stability balls, and exercise tubes, as well as posters demonstrating proper form and sample exercises.

+ Identify and mobilize the community (hospitals, YMCAs) and other partnerships (AHA and the International Health, Racquetball, and Sports Club Association (IHRSA)) to help address, support, and achieve goals.

+ The *International Association of Fire Fighters (IAFF)/ International Association of Fire Chiefs (IAFC) Fire Service Joint Labor Management Wellness-Fitness Initiative (WFI)*. The WFI is designed to be a holistic approach to firefighter health. It encompasses both fitness and medical evaluations, which give firefighters the information they need to make changes in lifestyle and habits that may contribute to poor health now and/or in the future. It is not designed to be punitive, but rather positive and reinforcing. Rehabilitation, behavioral health, and data collection are also vital parts of the program. The Peer Fitness Trainer (PFT) program has been very successful in that it "teaches our own" to "assist our own." This program is done in affiliation with the American Council on Exercise, but is customized for the fire service. Functional mobility exercises, core strengthening, and movement preparation are all parts of the training. It is becoming clearer that firefighters need to exercise in the same ways that they must perform. This allows their bodies to be adapted to the same movements that are required on an emergency scene (www.iafc.org/wfi; www.iaff.org).

+ The *Everyone Goes Home Firefighter Life Safety Initiatives* campaign developed by the National Fallen Firefighters Foundation (NFFF). These 16 life-safety initiatives provide a blueprint for effecting change within the fire service in an effort to prevent line-of-duty deaths and injuries (www.everyonegoeshome.com/initiatives.html).

+ The *National Fire Protection Association (NFPA)* (www.nfpa.org) and the Fire Department Safety Officers Association (www.fdsoa.org) have established standards, benchmarks, and related certifications that serve as resources for fire departments to create local programs for implementation.

+ The *Health and Wellness in the Volunteer Fire Service* guide produced by the NVFC and USFA, providing comprehensive information on fitness and wellness for volunteer firefighters and fire departments (www.nvfc.org). This guidebook includes examples of successful health and wellness programs that can be used in any department.

+ The *Best Practices in Emergency Vehicle Safe Operations for Volunteer and Small Combination Departments* report, produced by the NVFC in partnership with USFA, includes known practices, practical tools, and techniques to create a vehicle safety approach that will help departments manage the risk and loss to which they are exposed. This program includes a comprehensive self-assessment tool, allowing departments to look at each of the best practices and their major subcomponents, define them, and determine if they are already in place and if they are effective (NVFC, 2005).

Additionally, several States have combined community resources and partnerships to promote and achieve health, wellness, and safety initiatives. The fire service can tap into these resources to benefit firefighters and, in turn, the community. Examples include

+ **Maine**—established a grant initiative titled "Improving Care for Patients with Hypertension and High Cholesterol in the Primary Care Setting." This initiative provides funding to primary care sites to help patients control their high blood pressure and high blood cholesterol through patient and provider adherence to national guidelines (Improving Care, n.d.).

✚ **North Carolina**—works with the North Carolina Prevention Partners (NCPP) to increase preventive health benefits coverage that addresses high levels of blood pressure and cholesterol. The NCPP also trains employers and health plan managers to provide and improve disease management programs for treating high blood pressure, high cholesterol, and diabetes.

✚ **Mississippi and Ohio**—participate in the Know Your Numbers initiative, a public awareness campaign designed to increase people's knowledge of their blood cholesterol, glucose, blood pressure numbers, and body mass index (BMI). They have made the campaign culturally relevant for priority populations such as African-Americans and Hispanic-Americans.

✚ **Missouri**—collaborates with the St. Louis Fire Department to provide blood pressure and cholesterol screening, referral, and follow-up for inner-city residents.

✚ **Georgia**—provides education and assistance to the State's Chamber of Commerce. This effort resulted in one company's development of a strategic business and health plan titled "Seven Essential Elements in Risk Reduction." The same company also was able to partner with a hospital to conduct employee health screenings. Another company offered screening and risk reduction to more than 4,000 employees that resulted in a significant number of screened employees normalizing their blood cholesterol levels.

Step V. Creating a Supportive Environment is a long-term process that requires dedication to health, wellness, and safety values, creating a culture that supports safe and healthy behaviors. The first consideration is the physical look and feel of the department, i.e., the physical look, feel, smell, and sounds of the firehouse. In a supportive environment, people believe that the organization provides them with encouragement, opportunity, and rewards for healthy lifestyles and safety practices. The spirit that results is contagious. Suggested strategies for creating a supportive environment include

✚ vending machines with healthy choices;

✚ physical fitness areas;

✚ no smoking policies;

✚ relationships with local fitness clubs/networks for discounted memberships;

✚ healthy lifestyle and safe practices award recognition at conferences, awards banquets, etc.;

✚ introduction of interventions and safety procedures in firefighter orientation packets; and

✚ encourage, enforce, and reward compliance with all safety and health-related SOPs.

Step VI. Consistently Evaluating Outcomes determines the value of what has been achieved by evaluating the cost and desirability of the outcome.

Evaluations are important in order to:

✚ determine if the interventions worked;

✚ determine the cost benefit of the interventions;

✚ compare different types of interventions and their effectiveness; and

✚ provide information about the program to senior leaders and participants.

If the other steps have been established—senior level support, a good health, wellness, and safety team/committee, measurable goals and objectives outlined, and interventions implemented according to plan—then evaluating the programs will be a natural step in the process.

Examples

The following are examples of other "communities" with programs that incorporate the seven-step approach in their health, wellness, or safety initiatives:

➕ The Commonwealth of Virginia integrates health into the work culture through their CommonHealth wellness program. This program provides employees at high risk for Type-2 diabetes with a diabetes education program, an exercise program, health screenings, and weight management classes.

➕ General Motors (GM) provides a comprehensive health and wellness program for over one million GM employees, retirees, and dependents. The program, Lifesteps, sponsors health fairs, screenings, support classes, and an interactive Web site, *www.lifesteps.com*. As a result of this initiative, GM has reduced health risks as well as reduced the number of employees in its high-risk population.

➕ The Home Depot has established a companywide flu prevention program titled Building Better Health. This program has been successful in saving more than $460,000 in health-care expenditures and lost productivity.

➕ The State of Arkansas, led by Governor Mike Huckabee, launched a public awareness campaign on the benefits of not smoking, increasing exercise, and maintaining a healthy body weight.

Arkansas is also the first State in the Nation to measure the BMI of school children in order to create a baseline data source on the general health of its children.

➕ The Dow Chemical Company focuses on prevention through its Good Health for the Whole Self program. This program offers a variety of options: group programs, one-on-one counseling, home-based programs, and/or self-managed programs. Participants in the self-managed program, Positive Action, had significantly fewer medical claims than nonparticipants.

Similarly, the issues identified regarding operational safety aspects need a comprehensive strategy and action plan to address the challenges posed in safely responding to incidents, dealing with and managing the incident, and returning to the station. Two major components, a Safety Officer job description and a comprehensive, vehicle-safety program, are provided as Appendices 1 and 2 respectively.

Equipment use and maintenance guidelines should be developed according to the equipment manufacturer's recommendations. Each organization should also develop guidelines for assuring no firefighter is subjected to a situation where no life-saving objectives exist and there is minimal potential for saving significant property.

Summary

In order to decrease the number of sudden cardiac deaths and the onset of other chronic diseases in firefighters, as well as to ensure the safety of our Nation's first responders, it is imperative to institute a comprehensive health, wellness, and safety initiative. An effective initiative can be achieved by following three steps.

1 First, you must communicate to all firefighters the purpose and implementation of the health, wellness, and safety initiative. The message should be clear and concise and come from all stakeholders collectively. Success in any initiative is reduced when individual stakeholders attack the same problem at different times or with competing messages. By coordinating efforts and working together, you greatly increase the impact of your message.

2 Second, a comprehensive action plan for instituting the health, wellness, and safety initiative must be established. This plan should include appropriate interventions for lowering cholesterol and blood-pressure levels, increasing physical activity, maintaining a healthy weight, and promoting safe practices. Benchmarks of the plan include goals and objectives and that are measurable. This way outcomes and progress can be tracked.

3 Finally, firefighters must recognize that their health is a priority—and the number-one safety issue facing the fire service today. Occupational safety practices also must be in place to assure a safe working environment. Until firefighters begin to incorporate positive, healthy behaviors and use standardized safety practices, it will be difficult to meet the goals and objectives identified in this publication.

Next Steps

Healthy People 2010 established 10 Leading Health Indicators (LHIs) to measure the health of the Nation (HHS, 2005). They include physical activity; overweight and obesity; tobacco use; substance abuse; responsible sexual behavior; mental health; injury and violence; environmental quality; immunization; and access to health care. This joint NVFC/USFA project addressed LHIs as they relate to the risks for cardiovascular disease such as physical activity and overweight and obesity, as heart attacks continue to be leading cause of death among firefighters.

As mentioned earlier, firefighting is a hazardous job that exposes firefighters to a number of occupational risks, such as smoke and chemical inhalation, sleep deprivation, injury, and emotional stress (Rosenstock and Olsen, 2007). Future recommendations include an expansion of the NVFC Foundation's questionnaire to include questions about these risks and to establish goals and objectives as they relate to mental health, injury and violence, and environmental quality. Further discussion also should include access to health care. This study should pay close attention to volunteer firefighters who may continue serving beyond the age of 50 and may not have ongoing fitness and health requirements, putting them at an increased risk for developing cardiovascular disease (Rosenstock and Olsen, 2007).

Appendix 1

Safety Officer

OBJECTIVE: Provide for the integration of safety into the tasks performed by personnel.

QUALIFICATIONS: Same as supervisory level for firefighting, plus completed a class in fire department safety operations.

TERM: Two years, nominated by the Chief, in concurrence with the Deputy Chief and Assistant Chiefs, and subsequently appointed by the Chief.

REPORTS TO: Chief-Fire and Rescue Services

JOB SPECIFICS:

1. Oversees safety at incidents and training, bringing items of concern to the attention of the Incident Commander (IC).

2. Conducts one safety training per quarter.

3. Develop, propose to management, and implement a safety program for the organization, applying NFPA 1500 in concept.

4. Propose Standard Operating Guidelines (SOGs) and new equipment, equipment changes (with justification) for purchase, or implementation to the Chief.

5. Perform accident investigation, review, and implement prevention programs under the direction of the Officer-in-Charge.

6. Manage information related to accidents and identify problems and trends, proposing necessary action to the Chief.

7. This position holds no fireground authority other than safety-related issues.

NOTE: The Safety Officer can appoint up to two Assistant Safety Officers, upon concurrence with the Chief, with qualifications equal to his/hers.

ITEMS CAN BE ADDED OR CHANGED AS APPROPRIATE FOR YOUR FIRE DEPARTMENT

Appendix 2

Visit *www.nvfc.org* and visit the Resources page for the Emergency Vehicle Safe Operations for Volunteer and Small Combination Emergency Service Organizations guide.

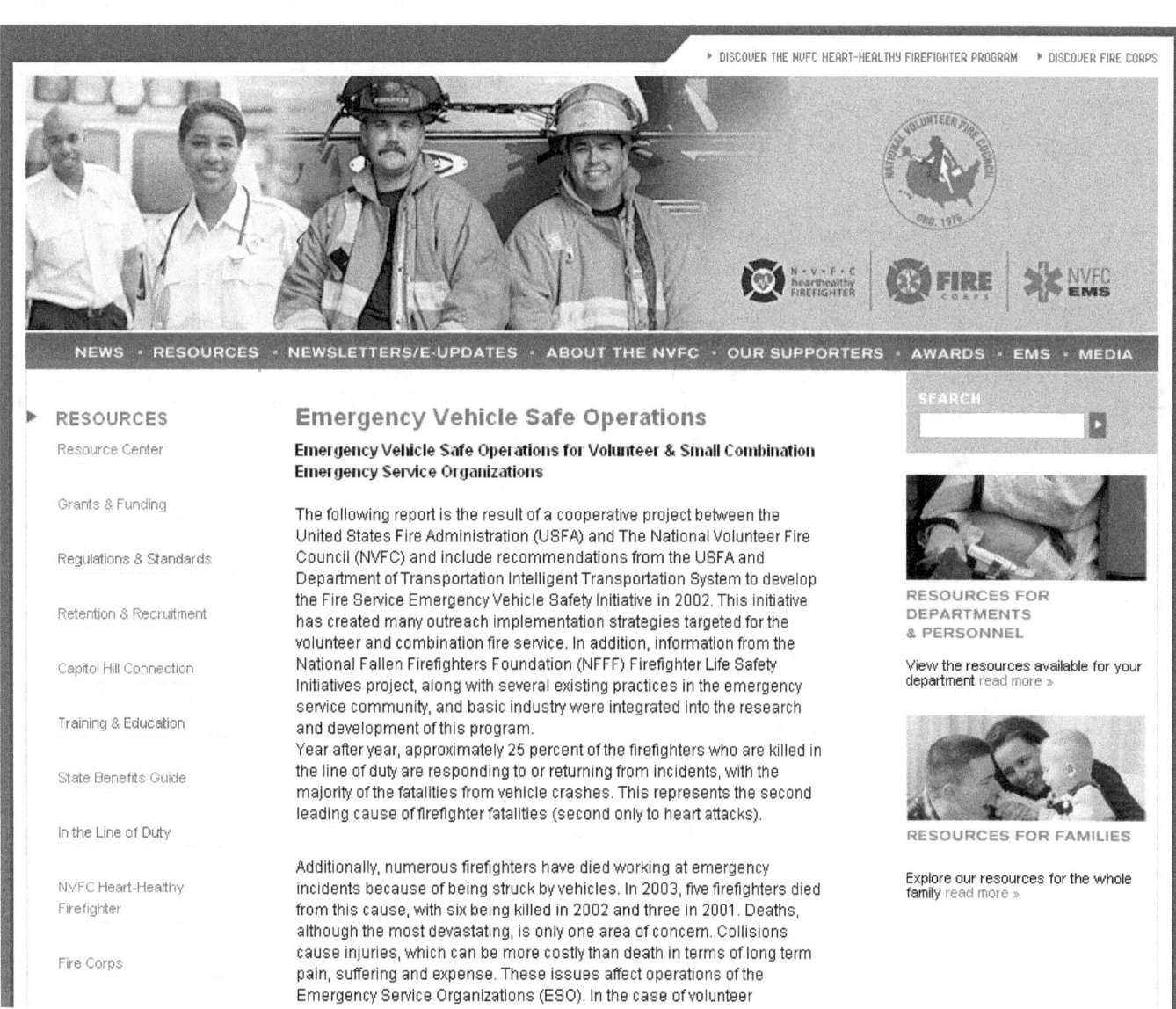

Terminology

ATHEROSCLEROSIS: hardening of the arteries, usually resulting from a buildup of cholesterol and other substances in the blood.

BLOOD PRESSURE: the force of blood against the artery walls.

CARDIOVASCULAR DISEASE: includes a variety of diseases of the heart and blood vessels, such as coronary heart disease and stroke.

CHOLESTEROL: a waxy substance that circulates in the bloodstream. Cholesterol comes from two sources: (1) it is manufactured in the liver, and (2) it comes from the foods you eat. When the level of cholesterol in the blood is too high, excess cholesterol is deposited in the artery walls. Over time, these deposits can build up, causing the arteries to narrow, thus reducing blood flow.

HEART ATTACK: also called acute myocardial infarction, occurs when a coronary artery becomes completely blocked resulting in a lack of blood flow to the heart muscle.

HEART DISEASE: the leading cause of death in the United States. Coronary heart disease is a specific name for the principal form of heart disease, the result of atherosclerosis or the buildup of cholesterol deposits in the coronary arteries that feed the heart.

HIGH BLOOD PRESSURE: a systolic blood pressure of 140 mmHg or greater or a diastolic blood pressure of 90 mmHg or greater. With high blood pressure, the heart has to work harder, resulting in an increased risk of heart attack or stroke.

HIGH CHOLESTEROL: desirable level of total cholesterol is less than 200 mg/dL. Borderline high (or higher risk) is between 200 and 239 mg/dL; high blood cholesterol (or two times the risk as the desirable level) is anything above 240 mg/dL.

METABOLIC SYNDROME: a condition diagnosed by the presence of three or more cardiovascular risk factors.

PLAQUE: buildup of cholesterol and calcium in the artery walls.

STROKE: a stroke occurs when a blood vessel bringing oxygen to the brain bursts or becomes clogged by a blood clot or some other particle. It is sometimes referred to as a "brain attack."

SUDDEN CARDIAC DEATH: sudden, unexpected death due to a loss of heart function. Sudden cardiac death is responsible for half of all heart disease deaths.

References

American Heart Association. *Heart Disease and Stroke Statistics:* 2006 Update, (Dallas, TX: American Heart Association, 2006).

American Heart Association. *Healthy Lifestyles Could Significantly Reduce High Blood Pressure,* January 2006. Retrieved April 23, 2007, from www.americanheart.org/ (no longer available).

American Heart Association (n.d.), *Alcohol, Wine and Cardiovascular Disease.* Retrieved April 23, 2007, from http://www.americanheart.org/presenter.jhtml?identifier=4422

Berlin, J.A. and Colditz, G.A. "A Meta-Analysis of Physical Activity in the Prevention of Coronary Heart Disease." *American Journal of Epidemiology* 132 (1990): 612-28.

Blair, S.N., Kohl III, H.W., Barlow, C.E., Paffenberger, Jr., R.S., et. al. "Changes in Physical Fitness and All-Cause Mortality: A Prospective Study of Healthy and Unhealthy Men." *Journal of the American Medical Association* 273 (1995):1093-96.

Booth, F.W. and Lees, S.J. "Fundamental Questions about Genes, Inactivity, and Chronic Diseases." *Physiological Genomics* 28 (2007): 146-57.

Brundtland, G.H., "Reducing Risks to Health, Promoting Healthy Life." *Journal of the American Medical Association* 288 (2002): 1974.

Centers for Disease Control and Prevention, Division for Heart Disease and Stroke Prevention (n.d.). *High Blood Cholesterol Prevention.* Retrieved April 23, 2007, from http://www.cdc.gov/cholesterol/prevention.htm

Centers for Disease Control and Prevention. *A Public Health Action Plan to Prevent Heart Disease and Stroke,* July 2003. Retrieved April 23, 2007, from http://www.cdc.gov/dhdsp/library/action_plan/pdfs/action_plan_full.pdf

Centers for Disease Control and Prevention, National Center for Health Statistics. *Healthy People 2000 Review,* 1998-99.

Centers for Disease Control and Prevention, National Center for Chronic Disease Prevention and Health Promotion. *Behavioral Risk Factor Surveillance System,* July 2007. Retrieved April 23, 2007, from http://www.cdc.gov/brfss/

Centers for Disease Control and Prevention, National Institute for Occupational Safety and Health, (n.d.). *Fire Fighter Fatality Investigation and Prevention Program Description.* Retrieved August 31, 2007, from http://www.cdc.gov/niosh/fire/implweb.html

Dunn, A.L., Marcus, B.H., Kampert, J.B., et. al. "Comparison of Lifestyle and Structured Interventions to Increase Physical Activity and Cardiorespiratory Fitness: A Randomized Trial." *Journal of the American Medical Association* 281 (1999): 327-34.

Fahy, R. *U.S. Firefighter Fatalities Due to Sudden Cardiac Death,* 1995-2004. Quincy, MA: National Fire Protection Association, 2005.

Manson, J.A., et. al. "A Prospective Study of Walking as Compared with Vigorous Exercise in the Prevention of "Coronary Heart Disease in Women." *New England Journal of Medicine* 341 (1999): 650-8.

Maine Cardiovascular Health Program (n.d.). *Improving Care for Patients with Hypertension and High Cholesterol in the Primary Care Setting.* Retrieved April 23, 2007, from http://www.mainecardiohealth.org/

National Ag Safety Database, Clemson Extension (n.d.). *Stress Management for the Health of It.* Retrieved April 23, 2007, from http://www.cdc.gov/nasd/docs/d001201-d001300/d001245/d001245.html

National Center for Chronic Disease Prevention and Health Promotion, Centers for Disease Control and Prevention. *Preventing Heart Disease and Stroke: Addressing the Nation's Leading Killers.* CDC At-A-Glance Report. Atlanta: U.S. Department of Health and Human Services, 2005.

National Diabetes Information Clearinghouse. National Diabetes Statistics, November 2005. Retrieved April 23, 2007, from http://diabetes.niddk.nih.gov/dm/pubs/statistics/index.htm

National Institute of Diabetes and Digestion and Kidney Disease, National Institute of Health, National Diabetes Information Clearinghouse (n.d.). *Can Type-2 Diabetes Be Prevented?* Retrieved April 23, 2007, from http://diabetes.niddk.nih.gov/dm/pubs/riskfortype2/

National Institute on Drug Abuse, National Institute of Health. Retrieved April 23, 2007, from http://www.nida.nih.gov/

National Safety Council, *Accident Prevention Manual for Industrial Operations* (Chicago: National Safety Council, 1978).

National Volunteer Fire Council, Fired Up For Fitness (n.d.). *More about the Program.* Retrieved April 23, 2007, from http://challenge.healthy-firefighter.org/about/default.aspx

National Volunteer Fire Council, *Emergency Vehicle Safe Operations for Volunteer and Small Combination Emergency Service Organizations,* 2005. Retrieved August 13, 2007, from http://nvfc.org/page/988/Emergency_Vehicle_Safe_Operations.htm

O'Connor, G.T., Henekens, C.H., Willett W.H., et. al. "Physical Exercise and Reduced Risk of Nonfatal Myocardial Infarction." *American Journal of Epidemiology* 142 (1995): 1147-56.

O'Donnell, M.P. and Ainsworth, T. *Health Promotion in the Workplace.* New York: John Wiley and Sons, 1984.

Partnership for Prevention. *Leading by Example Initiative* (n.d.). *Leading by Example. Improving the Bottom Line through a High Performance, Less Costly Workforce.* Washington, D.C.: Partnership for Prevention.

Pate, R.R., Pratt, M., Blair, S.N., et. al. "Physical Activity and Public Health: A Recommendation for the Centers for Disease Control and Prevention and the American College of Sports Medicine." *Journal of the American Medical Association* 273 (1995): 402-7.

Peregrin, T. "Weighing in on Corporate Wellness Programs and Their Impact on Obesity." *Journal of the American Dietetic Association* 105 (2005): 1192.

Physical Activity and Cardiovascular Health. "NIH Consensus Development Panel on Physical Activity and Cardiovascular Health." *Journal of the American Medical Association* 276, no. 3 (1996): 241-6.

"Position of the American Dietetic Association: Optimal Weight as a Health Promotion Strategy." *Journal of the American Dietetic Association* 89 (December 1989): 1814-17.

"Position of the American Dietetic Association: The Role of Nutrition in Health Promotion and Disease Prevention Programs," *Journal of the American Dietetic Association* 98 (February 1998): 205-8.

Rosenstock, L., Olsen, J. "Firefighting and Death from Cardiovascular Causes." *New England Journal of Medicine* 356 (March 2007): 12.

Schult, T.M., McGovern, P.M., Dowd, B., and Pronk, P. "The Future of Health Promotion/Disease Prevention Programs: The Incentives and Barriers Faced by Stockholders." *Journal of Occupational and Environmental Medicine* 48 (2006): 541.

The Wellness Councils of America (n.d.). "Seven Benchmarks of Success." Retrieved April 23, 2007, from http://www.welcoa.org/wellworkplace/index.php?category=2

Tribal Justice Information Sharing System. Glossary of Terms, 2004. Retrieved June 15, 2007, from http://www.tjiss.net/glossary_b.html

United States Department of Health and Human Services. *Healthy People 2010,* ed., in two volumes. (Washington, D.C.: January 2000).

United States Department of Health and Human Services. *A Public Health Action Plan to Prevent Heart Disease and Stroke: Executive Summary and Overview.* Atlanta, GA: U.S. Department of Health and Human Services, Centers for Disease Control and Prevention, 2003.

United States Department of Health and Human Resources, Office of Disease Prevention and Health Promotion. *Healthy People 2010,* 2005.

United States Department of Homeland Security, Federal Emergency Management Agency. *Firefighter Fatalities in the United States in 2003.* Washington, D.C.: United States Fire Administration, August 2004.

United States Fire Administration, Federal Emergency Management Agency. *Firefighters.* December 2006. Retrieved April 23, 2007, from http://www.usfa.dhs.gov/statistics/firefighters/index.shtm

United States Fire Administration. *Firefighter Fatality Retrospective Study,* EME-2000-DO-0396. Washington, D.C.: U.S. Government Printing Office, 2004.

United States Fire Administration. "USFA Firefighter Fatality Reports and Statistics." 12 January 2004. Retrieved August 13, 2007, from http://www.usfa.dhs.gov/fireservice/fatalities/statistics/index.shtm

United States Fire Administration. 2006 *Annual Report,* 2006. Retrieved August 14, 2007, from http://www.usfa.dhs.gov/fireservice/fatalities/statistics/report.shtm

VFIS, *Firefighter Safety.* York, PA: VFIS, 2000.

Warburton, D.E., Nicol, C.W., and Bredin, S.D. "Health Benefits of Physical Activity: The Evidence." *Canadian Medical Association Journal* 174 (2006): 801-9.

Whitney, E. and Rolfes, S.R. *Understanding Nutrition,* 11th ed. Belmont, CA: Thomson Wadsworth Publishing, 2008.

Willett, W.H., Dietz, W.H., and Colditz, G.A. "Primary Care: Guidelines for Healthy Weight." *New England Journal of Medicine* 341 (1999): 427-34.